Mapping the UK

MAPPING
MOUNTAINS

Louise Spilsbury

Heinemann
LIBRARY

www.heinemann.co.uk/library
Visit our website to find out more information about Heinemann Library books.

To order:
 Phone 44 (0) 1865 888066
 Send a fax to 44 (0) 1865 314091
Visit the Heinemann Bookshop at www.heinemann.co.uk/library to browse our catalogue and order online.

First published in Great Britain by Heinemann Library, Halley Court, Jordan Hill, Oxford OX2 8EJ, part of Harcourt Education.
Heinemann is a registered trademark of Harcourt Education Ltd.

© Harcourt Education Ltd 2005
The moral right of the proprietor has been asserted.

Editorial: Lucy Thunder and Harriet Milles
Design: Ron Kamen and Celia Jones
Illustrations: Barry Atkinson, Darren Lingard and Jeff Edwards
Picture Research: Melissa Allison and Beatrice Ray
Production: Camilla Smith

Originated by Repro Multi Warna
Printed and bound in China WKT Company Limited

The paper used to print this book comes from sustainable resources.

ISBN 0 431 01325 X
09 08 07 06 05
10 9 8 7 6 5 4 3 2 1

British Library Cataloguing in Publication Data

Spilsbury, Louise
(Mapping the UK). – Mapping Mountains
526'.09143

A full catalogue record for this book is available from the British Library.

Acknowledgements
The Publishers would like to thank the following for permission to reproduce photographs:
Alamy Images pp. 5, 7t; Corbis Royalty-Free pp. 10 (woodland and scree), 25 (Himalayas); Get Mapping pp. 8, 18; Getty Images p. 22; Getty Images/Photodisc pp. 10 (Loch Ness and slope), 24 (Rocky Mountains, Andes, globe), 26; Harcourt Education Ltd/Peter Evans pp. 10 (stream), 7b, 20; istockphoto.com pp. 6, 25, (Alps, Atlas); Jane Hance p. 10 (footpath, outcrop, boulders, marsh, camp site, information centre, car park); Photomap p. 13; Reproduced by permission of Ordnance Survey on behalf of The Controller of Her Majesty's Stationery Office, © Crown Copyright 100000230 pp.15, 17, 19, 21b, 21t; Simmons Aerofilms p. 14.

Cover photograph of Snowdonia in North Wales, reproduced with permission of Harcourt Education Ltd/Peter Evans. Section of Ordnance Survey map reproduced by permission of Ordnance Survey on behalf of The Controller of Her Majesty's Stationery Office, © Crown Copyright 100000230.

The Publishers would like to thank Dr Margaret Mackintosh, Honorary Editor of *Primary Geographer*, for her assistance in the preparation of this book.

Every effort has been made to contact copyright holders of any material reproduced in this book. Any omissions will be rectified in subsequent printings if notice is given to the Publishers.

Contents

What are maps?...4

Looking at mountains 6

Marking mountains on maps 8

Mapping symbols 10

Up and down mountains............................12

Climb Ben Nevis! 14

Using directions and grids 16

Visit the Lake District 18

A sense of scale..20

Mountains of the UK 22

Going global..24

Mountain bike mayhem!............................26

Quick-stop map skills...............................28

Map skills answers 29

Glossary...30

Find out more..31

Index 32

Words appearing in the text in bold, **like this**, are explained in the Glossary.

▶ Look out for this symbol! When you see it next to a question, you will find the answer on page 29.

What are maps?

Have you ever walked on a hillside or a mountain? Did you, your family or friends use a map to find your way there? Maps are special drawings of places in the world. They are usually drawn on flat paper. Maps show us where things are and help us to find our way around.

Looking down from above

Imagine you are in a hot-air balloon, floating high in the sky and looking straight down on some mountains below. This overhead view is called an **aerial** view – and this is how maps show us the world. Objects and features look very different when you look at them from above. Buildings look like rectangles and trees look like circles. How would your school buildings look from above?

Hi! I'm Carta – and I'm coming along for some mountain mapping mayhem! Let's find out how useful and interesting maps can be.

Below is a simple map of a car park area at the bottom of a mountain. Walkers park here, and they can buy maps from the Tourist Information Centre. This map shows how the area looks from above. Can you imagine how it might look in real life?

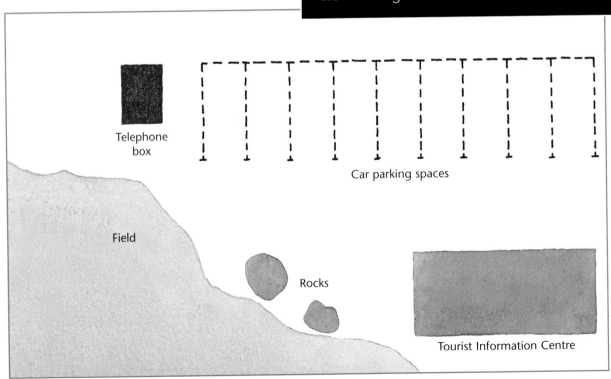

Telephone box

Car parking spaces

Field

Rocks

Tourist Information Centre

Have a go!

A good way to help you to understand maps is to draw one yourself. Try drawing a simple map, like the one on the opposite page. You could draw your bedroom. Just imagine you are a fly on the ceiling, looking down on the room. Only include the **permanent features** – the things that are in the same place all the time. A map of a landscape would include roads and buildings, but not people or cars.

A mapping adventure

This book takes you on a mapping adventure up mountains. You will learn how to read maps, and use them to find out about the features of mountains. Maps can also help you to find your way around many other different places.

It is easy to get lost in hills or mountains, so you should always use a map to find your way around.

Looking at mountains

In the UK, any high ground that measures more than 600 metres above sea level is usually called a mountain. Hills are lower. Mountains often have a prominent, rocky top called a **peak**, whereas hilltops are generally more rounded.

Mountain features

As you get higher up a mountain, it gets colder and windier. This affects what will grow at the different levels. There are usually trees growing on the lower levels of a mountain, unless they have been cut down to clear land for farming. Climbing up, you reach **moorland** level, where there are fewer trees. Low-growing plants, such as tough grasses and heather, are found here. These plants stay closer to the ground, out of the path of cold winds. On mountain tops, there may be snow in winter. There are no trees here, but plants may grow in cracks in the rocks, where they are sheltered from the weather.

The height of a mountain or hill is measured from the average level of the sea to the highest peak. The highest mountain in the UK is Ben Nevis, at 1,344 metres high. This means that its height measures 1,344 metres above sea level.

The wind-blasted moorland or mid-level of a mountain often looks like this. There are few trees. Mostly grasses and other tough plants grow there.

Some mountain tops are so high that they may be covered in ice and snow all year round.

The lower levels of a mountain may be covered in trees.

Marking mountains on maps

Mapmakers have to take detailed measurements of the **permanent features** on the ground in order to make maps. They also use photographs taken from aeroplanes or **satellites**. These are called **aerial** photographs. Here we are going to make a map from a real aerial photograph.

Looking down on a mountain

An area where there are several mountains close together in a line is called a mountain **range**. The separate **peaks** of a mountain range may be joined together by a long narrow stretch of rocky land called a **ridge**.

Rivers and valleys

The rain water that falls on high ground runs into streams. These streams run down mountain sides and join up to form rivers. Most mountains have **valleys** in between them. Valleys are deep grooves in the land that have been carved out of the rock by rivers or **glaciers**. Lakes or **lochs** form in dips or hollows in the mountain rock where water gathers.

This is an aerial view of the **summit** of Mount Snowdon in Wales. The blue patches are lakes. The dark patches are steep slopes.

Mapping a mountain

The tricky thing about drawing mountains on a map is how to show their height. One way of showing high ground on a map is by using colour. On this map, the lowest areas of land are yellow; the higher areas of land are coloured in shades of brown. The darkest brown areas are the highest. Rivers and streams flowing down from high ground, sometimes into lakes, are shown as blue lines.

Maps that show the natural features of a landscape, such as mountains and rivers, in shades of colour are called 'physical' or 'shaded relief' maps.

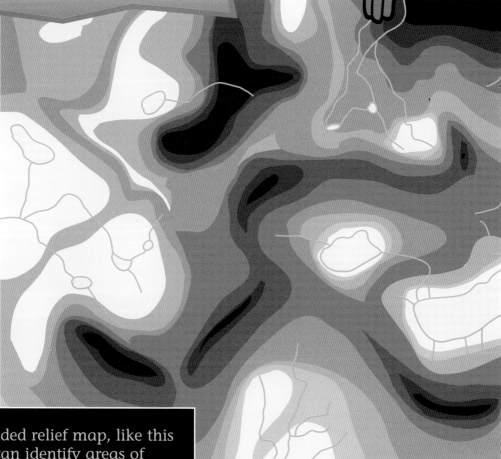

On a shaded relief map, like this one, we can identify areas of mountains and hills by the brown shading.

Mapping symbols

There is not enough space on most maps to draw detailed pictures of every feature. Instead, mapmakers use symbols. Map symbols are pictures, shapes, lines or even letters that represent real objects or features. For example, all rivers on maps are drawn as blue lines, and forests are shown as patches of green with little tree picture symbols.

Symbol secrets

The map symbols on this page represent some of the things you might find on mountains and hills. Many of the natural features have been created by **erosion** by wind, water, ice, or people. **Scree** is the name for small, loose stones on mountain slopes. It is made by frost shattering rocks into pieces. **Rocky outcrops** are large lumps of harder rock that are left sticking out when patches of softer rock around them have been eroded.

These are some of the symbols used to represent mountain and hill features on maps. When you draw a map, try to make up some of your own symbols!

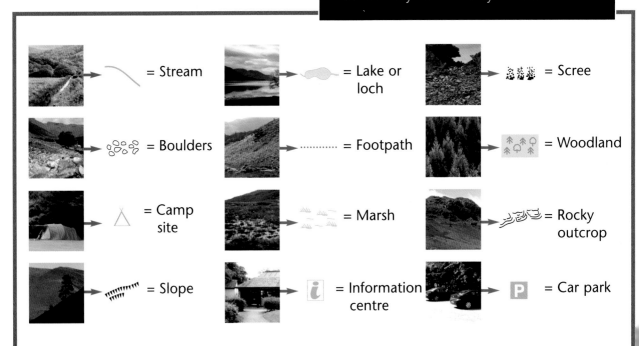

= Stream

= Boulders

= Camp site

= Slope

= Lake or loch

= Footpath

= Marsh

= Information centre

= Scree

= Woodland

= Rocky outcrop

= Car park

> A map key (or legend) tells you what all the symbols on a map mean. It helps you to unlock a map's secrets!

Other mountain symbols

People use mountains in many different ways. Forestry companies grow trees on mountains so that they can harvest the wood. Water companies build **reservoirs**, and pipe the water from them to towns and cities. Many people visit mountains and hills to go skiing, climbing, mountain biking, and walking. On many maps there are symbols to represent some of the features connected with these activities – for instance, camp sites, car parks, mountain rescue centres, and footpaths.

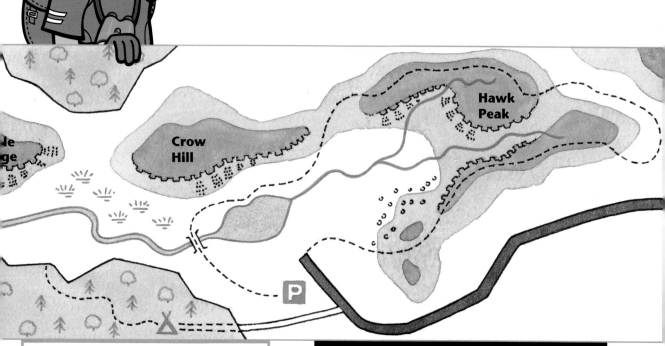

KEY

🌉	Bridge	〰️	River
▬	Road	⬭	Lake
P	Parking	🌿	Marsh
-----	Footpath	🪨	Woodland
⛺	Camp site		
	Scree	° ° °	Boulders

○ Using the map symbols and key, can you describe where the camp site is on this map? Which mountains or hills have scree at their bases?

Up and down mountains

Some mountains have gently sloping sides and large areas of flat land on top. Others are rugged and high, with rocky **peaks**, steep sides and deep **valleys** running down them. The **gradient** of a hill or mountain is the steepness of its slopes. How are gradients shown on maps?

Counting on contours

Many maps use contour lines to show the height of the land. These help us to work out how steep the slopes are. Contour lines join up bits of land that are the same height above sea level. The diagram below will help you to understand how contour lines work.

Contour lines are tricky to understand! Just remember that when the lines are drawn close together it means that a slope is steep. When contour lines are far apart, the slopes are gentler and the land is flatter. Maps can also show when roads or trails are steep by using gradient arrow symbols, like this >>>.

The lower part of this diagram shows two mountains from the side. We have drawn contour lines up the mountains at every 50 metres. The contour lines wrap all the way round the mountains. The top part of the diagram shows you how the contour lines would look on a map. ◗Which mountain has the steepest slope?

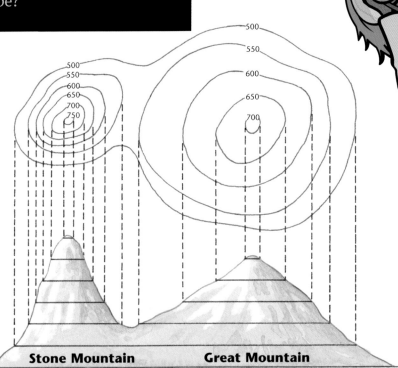

750m —
700m —
650m —
600m —
550m —
500m —
Sea level —

Stone Mountain   **Great Mountain**

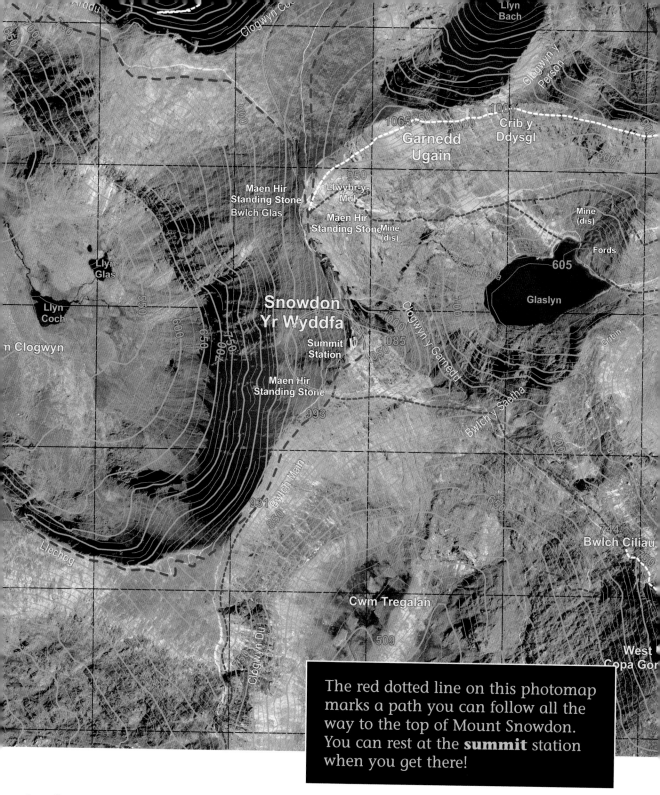

The red dotted line on this photomap marks a path you can follow all the way to the top of Mount Snowdon. You can rest at the **summit** station when you get there!

A photomap of Snowdon

The photomap above shows Mount Snowdon in Wales. The mapmaker has used a real **aerial** photograph of the area and labelled some of the features. There are also contour lines linking up land that is exactly the same height. The numbers by the contour lines give the height of the land in metres.

Climb Ben Nevis!

Ben Nevis is a mountain in the Grampian mountain **range** that runs through the centre of Scotland. The **peak** of Ben Nevis is so high and cold that it is covered with snow even in the summer months. We are going to look at a photograph of Ben Nevis and a map of the area to see what we can find out about this famous mountain.

Always be safe when climbing any mountain or hill, especially Ben Nevis! Check the weather forecasts before you go. Take a map, be sure that you know how to use it, and keep to the paths. Remember that the weather on high ground can change quickly. Take food, drink and also clothing to protect you from cold, wind and rain.

Ben Nevis is very popular with walkers and climbers. One side is so steep that only skilled mountaineers can climb it. On the other side there are paths that almost anyone can follow. Can you see the paths in this photo?

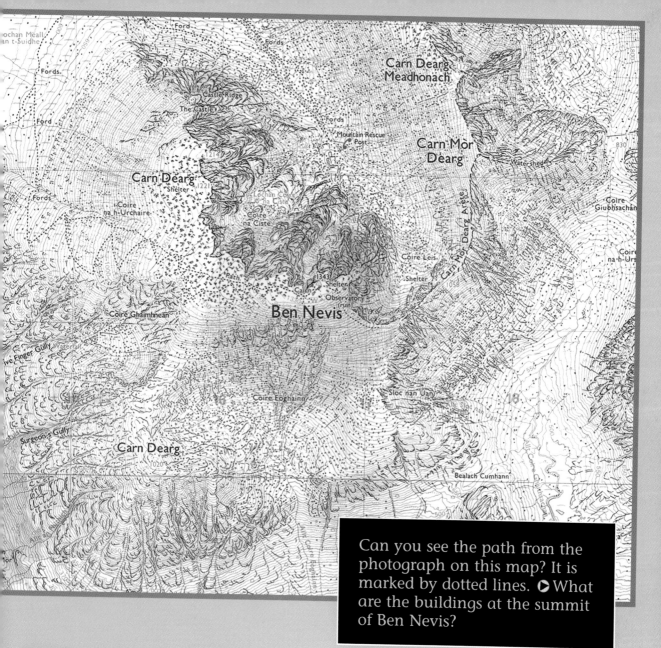

Can you see the path from the photograph on this map? It is marked by dotted lines. ▷What are the buildings at the summit of Ben Nevis?

Discovering Ben Nevis

The map on this page is a section of an **Ordnance Survey** map of Ben Nevis. The pink lines are contour lines. The steepest parts of the mountain look almost red on this map, because the contour lines are so close together. The **summit** of Ben Nevis is flatter, so the contour lines here are wider apart.

Can you see the **rocky outcrops** and the areas of boulders and **scree** on the map? (It may help to look back at the symbols pictures on page 10.) The rainwater that falls on the mountain collects in streams. These are shown as blue lines on the map. As they flow into **valleys** down the mountainside, they feed into rivers and lakes.

Using directions and grids

Directions help us to find places or features. Maps use compass directions – north, east, south, and west. Most maps are drawn with north at the top. In the map below, Hawk Peak lies east of Crow Hill.

Using grids

Grid references are a more exact way of locating a feature or place. Many maps have sets of lines that form grid squares. In the map below, the lines going up (vertically) have different letters. The lines going across (horizontally) have numbers. A grid reference is the letter and number that mark a square. To read a grid reference, we give the letter on the vertical lines first and then the number on the horizontal line. (Remember this by the phrase: 'Along the corridor and up the stairs.') So in this map, the camp site is in D,1 and Hawk Peak is in I,4.

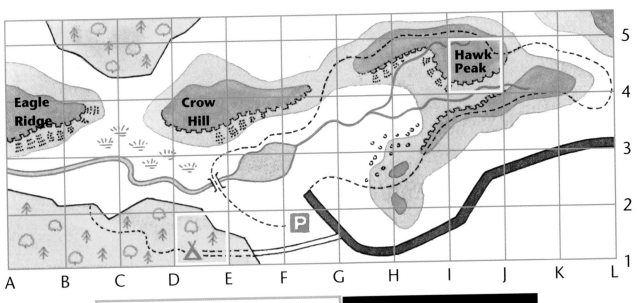

KEY

Bridge		River	
Road		Lake	
Parking		Marsh	
Footpath		Woodland	
Camp site		Boulders	
Scree			

▶ Can you work out the grid reference for the car park? Which hill or mountain is at grid reference D,3?

Mapping Cadair Idris

The **Ordnance Survey** map on this page shows part of the area around Cadair Idris, a mountain in Wales. Ordnance Survey maps have grids with numbers on both the vertical and horizontal lines. On this map, the grid reference for Llyn (Lake) Cau is 71, 12. The area called 'The Saddle' is in grid square 70, 13.

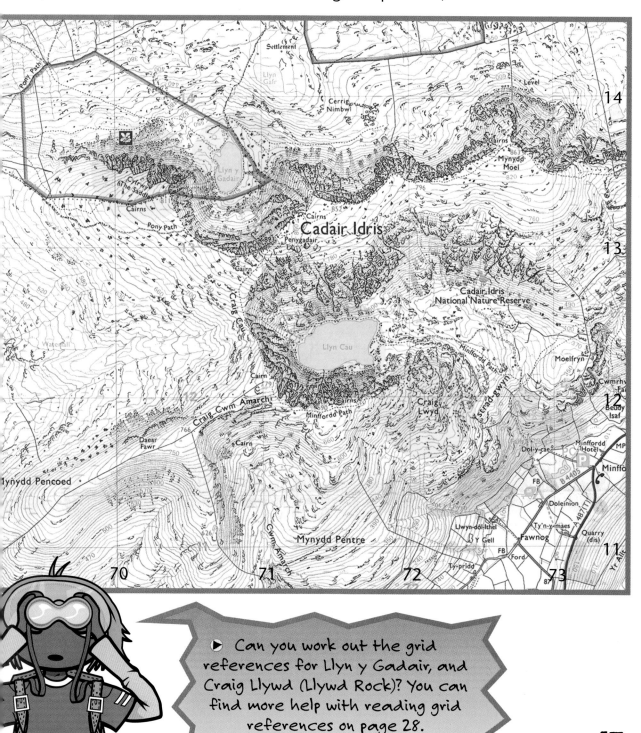

▶ Can you work out the grid references for Llyn y Gadair, and Craig Llywd (Llywd Rock)? You can find more help with reading grid references on page 28.

Visit the Lake District

The Lake District is a **National Park** in northwest England, in the county of Cumbria. It has wild and beautiful mountains, dotted with lakes, **moorland** and woodland. Around 12 million people go there every year to enjoy the scenery.

Hardknott Pass

The **aerial** photograph below shows the area around Hardknott Pass in the Lake District. Hardknott Pass is the long, wiggly, white road you can see going across the middle of the photo. It is famous because it is the steepest road in England! Long ago, the area around the Pass was covered in woodland. These trees were cut down to clear land for farming. The forest you can see poking in at the bottom of the picture is full of conifer trees, which people plant and later cut down for timber.

This is a vertical aerial view of Hardknott Pass. It was taken from an aeroplane high in the air and looks straight down from above.

Map-reading

The map on this page is a section of **Ordnance Survey** map of the Hardknott Pass area. On the map the road is shown as a yellow line and the **gradient** arrow symbols show that it is steep. The map is also useful because it can tell you what different features are called.

Straight above the forest on the other side of this Pass is Border End. This area has lots of **rocky outcrop** symbols close together. Can you spot this rocky area on the photo too? In the bottom right-hand corner of the map is the River Duddon. There are no contour lines or rocky symbols here because around the river are flat fields. Can you see the river and fields in the bottom right-hand corner of the photo?

On an Ordnance Survey map each grid square represents one square kilometre of land in real life. For example, by using the grid squares on the map below, you can work out that Yew Crags are approximately two kilometres from Dod Pike. ▶ Can you work out roughly how far it is between Black Hall and Border End?

We have put 'spotlights' on this map to help you find places and features more easily.

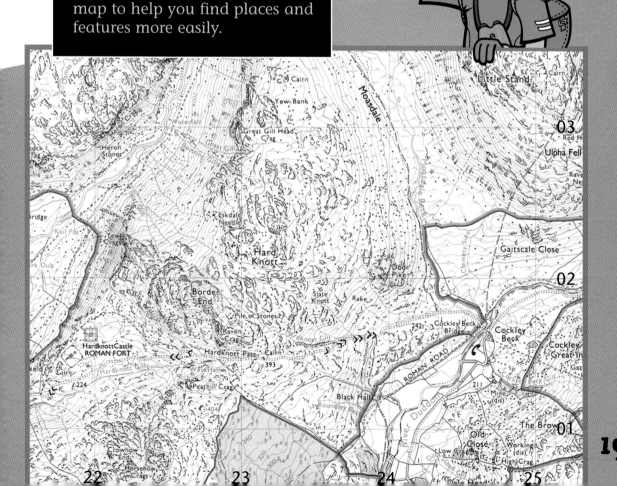

A sense of scale

Maps can show many different things. Some maps focus on particular subjects or themes. For example, a weather forecast map uses symbols to show the weather expected for different places. One of the main differences you will notice about most of the maps you will use is their scale.

A large-scale map shows a small area of land in a lot of detail. A small-scale map shows a bigger area of land, but with less detail.

Understanding scale

It is pretty obvious that maps cannot show things at their actual size! Maps are 'scaled down' in size. This means that everything is drawn much smaller on a map than it is in real life. The scale of a map is a number that tells you how much smaller something is on a map compared to real life. A map's scale is usually shown on a scale bar. You can see a scale bar on the maps opposite. If the scale is 1:25 000, this means that 1 centimetre on the map is equal to 25,000 centimetres (or 250 metres) in real life.

The **summit** of Mount Snowdon is 1,085 metres high, making it the highest mountain in Wales. Snowdon is found in Snowdonia **National Park**.

Looking at map scales

To see how scale works, take a look at the two maps of the area around Snowdon on this page. ▶ Which map would be better for walkers to use if they wanted to climb Snowdon? Which map would be better for drivers to use to plan how to get to the area? Can you explain why?

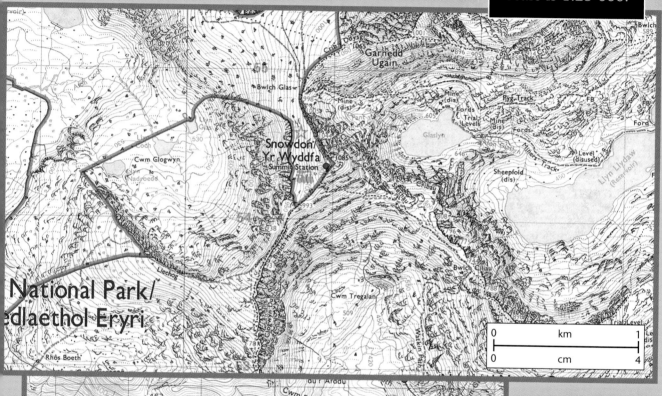

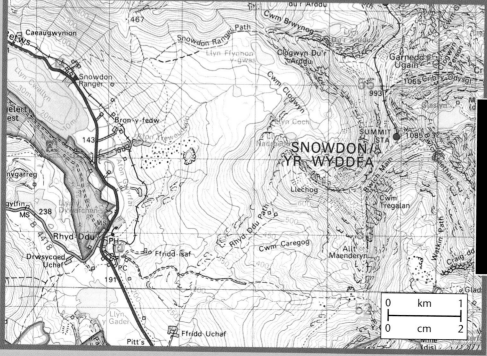

Mountains of the UK

Maps of large areas of land, such as the whole of the British Isles, are made using **satellite** photographs. These are special kinds of **aerial** photographs taken from a satellite circling the Earth in space.

As well as using photographs, mapmakers use **surveyors'** reports to make maps. Surveyors are people who take measurements and gather information about landscape features on the ground. For example, they would find out whether a particular area of ground on a hill was marshy or dry. Most mapmakers today use computers to bring all the information together to make a map.

The main areas of mountains in the UK are in the west and north of the country. In fact, over 70% (seven out of ten) of mountains in the UK are in Scotland!

This is a satellite picture of the British Isles.

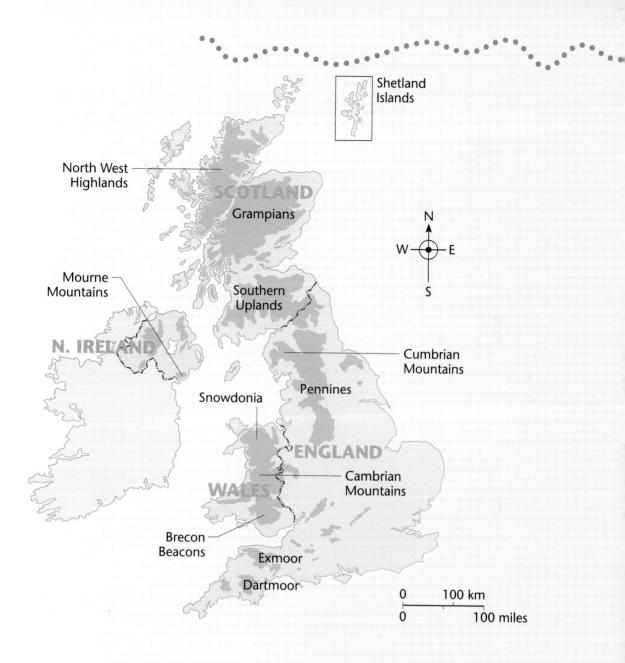

North West Highlands

SCOTLAND

Grampians

Shetland Islands

N
W — E
S

Mourne Mountains

Southern Uplands

N. IRELAND

Cumbrian Mountains

Snowdonia

Pennines

ENGLAND

Cambrian Mountains

WALES

Brecon Beacons

Exmoor

Dartmoor

0   100 km

0   100 miles

Mountain tourism

Tourism brings a lot of money to the mountain areas of the UK. This can have good and bad effects on these areas. For example, visitors spend money in local hotels, shops, restaurants, and ski resorts. Some of this money is used to manage and protect mountain areas. However, too many walkers, bikers, and skiers can **erode** the land – especially if they stray off the marked paths. People can also frighten wildlife, leave litter, and their cars cause air **pollution**.

This map shows the areas in the UK where the highest mountains and hills can be found. Can you see some of the mountain **ranges** that we have talked about in this book?

Going global

Mountains can be found in all the **continents** of the world. In fact, mountains cover almost a quarter of the Earth's land surface. Some are dramatic mountains that rise above the land in a single **peak**. Others are long **ranges** of mountains that extend for hundreds of kilometres.

Mountains on a globe

One way of looking at the mountains of the world is on a globe. A globe is a spherical (ball-shaped) map of the world. There are also flat maps of the world like the one on these pages. Look at the mountain ranges shown on this world map and then see if you can find them on a globe.

The fourteen highest mountains in the world are all in the Himalayan mountain range in central Asia. This includes Everest – the highest of all. At 8,848 metres, it is six and a half times higher than Ben Nevis!

Rocky Mountains

NORTH AMERICA

Sierra Madre

ATLANTIC OCEAN

The Rocky Mountains

SOUTH AMERICA

PACIFIC OCEAN

Andes

The Andes

The Earth is a giant rocky ball. A globe like this is a scaled-down model of the world.

A global problem

Across the world, people are damaging mountains. Mining companies dig out vast holes in mountainsides, and destroy wildlife **habitats**. People cut down trees on the lower slopes to make space for building or farming. Rainwater then washes some of the bare soil into rivers, making it dirty and unfit to use. The rivers that flow down from mountains supply half the people of the world with their water. Protecting the world's mountains is also about protecting the world's people!

The Alps

ARCTIC OCEAN

EUROPE
Alps

Ural Mountains

ASIA

PACIFIC OCEAN

The Himalayas

Atlas
Mountains

Himalayas

AFRICA

Ethiopian
Highlands

INDIAN
OCEAN

AUSTRALIA

OUTH
LANTIC
CEAN

The Atlas Mountains

SOUTHERN OCEAN

This map shows the continents, oceans, and some of the main mountain ranges of the world.

ANTARCTICA

25

Mountain bike mayhem!

Ready for some off-road cycling fun? Now that you know so much about maps, you can use your skills to ride a mountain bike around some mountain trails. To complete the trail correctly, all you need to do is collect the first letters of the features along the way to make up a word.

1 Start from the village of Hillview. There are two trails. Follow the trail going north for about 2 kilometres. What is the first letter of the name of the feature here?

2 Now pedal away to grid reference 43,28. What is the first letter of the name of the water feature here?

3 There are two tracks to choose from here (>>> or >). Take the steepest track heading southwards to a high point. What is the first letter of its name?

4 Keep cycling southwards down the path to the bridge that takes you over the river. What can you see to the west of the bridge? What is the first letter of the name of this hill?

5 Now cycle on to grid reference 46,24. What is the first letter of the name of the wood you are in?

6 Again, there are two tracks to choose from. Head southeast for just over 1 kilometre until you get to your last stop. What is the first letter of its name?

▶ If you put all the letters together, what word do you come up with?

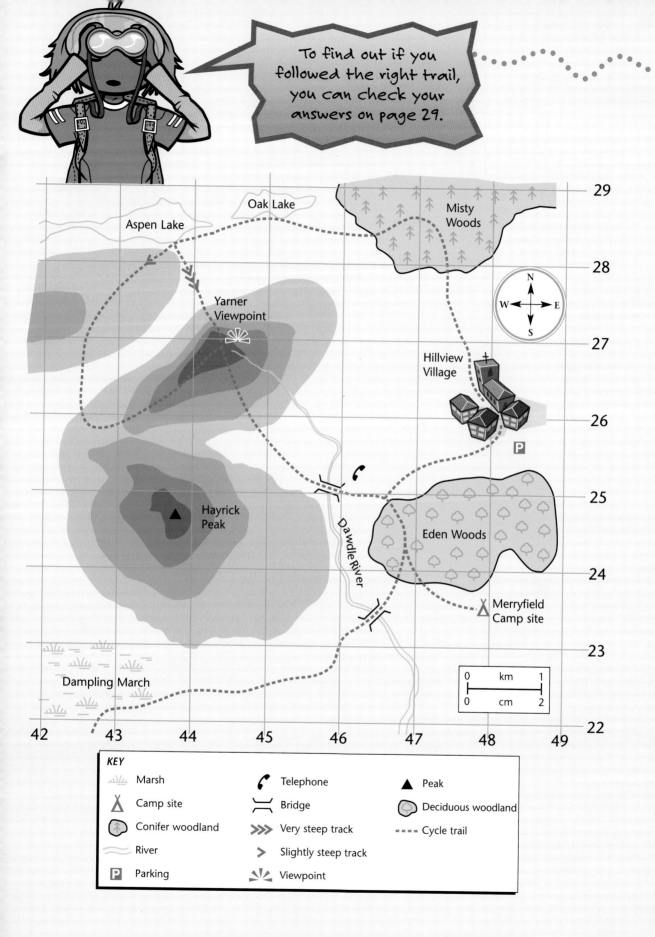

To find out if you followed the right trail, you can check your answers on page 29.

Quick-stop map skills

What are symbols?
Map symbols are pictures, letters, shapes, lines, or patterns that represent different features, such as rivers and roads. Map keys show what the symbols stand for.

Key

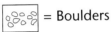 = Stream   = Boulders

How can I measure distances?
On **Ordnance Survey** maps, each grid square represents 1 kilometre, so you can roughly work out distance by counting grid squares.

What are grid references?
Grid references are numbers that locate a particular square on a map. To give a grid reference, you give the number on the vertical line first and then the number on the horizontal line. ('Along the corridor and up the stairs.')

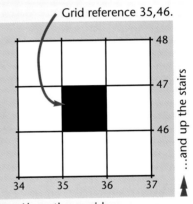

Grid reference 35,46.

...and up the stairs

Along the corridor...

How does scale work?
A map scale tells you how much smaller a feature is on a map than it is in real life. Everything on a map is scaled down in size. On a 1:25 000 scale map, things are 25,000 times smaller than real life.

How are slopes shown on a map?
Maps show slopes by using shaded colours, contour lines, or **gradient** arrows. Gradient arrows look like this >>>. The more arrows, the steeper the slope is. Contour lines join up areas of land that are the same height. When contour lines are close together the slope is steep. When contour lines are spaced out, the land is flatter. Numbers next to, or on the lines tell us the exact height of the land in metres.

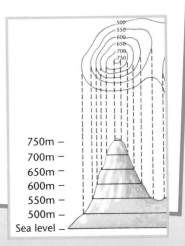

750m –
700m –
650m –
600m –
550m –
500m –
Sea level –

Map skills answers

Page 11: The camp site is in the woods. There is **scree** at the bottom of Crow Hill, Hawk Peak and Eagle Ridge.

Page 12: Stone Mountain has the steepest slopes. We know this because the contour lines are closer together on this mountain.

Page 15: The buildings at the **summit** of Ben Nevis are a shelter and the ruins of an observatory.

Page 16: The grid reference for the car park is F,1. The hill or mountain at grid reference D,3 is Crow Hill.

Page 17: The grid reference for Llyn y Gadair is 70,13 and the grid reference for Craig Llywd (Llywd Rock) is 72,11.

Page 19: The distance between Black Hall and Border End is approximately 1.25 kilometres.

Page 21: Walkers would use the 1:25 000 large-scale map (top) for walking on Snowdon, because it shows the footpaths and contour lines more clearly. Drivers would use the 1:50 000 small-scale map (bottom). This is because the map shows a larger area of land – and the roads that will take them to the area from further away.

Page 26–27: 1 – M (<u>M</u>isty Woods); 2 – A (<u>A</u>spen Lake); 3 – Y (<u>Y</u>arner Viewpoint); 4 – H (<u>H</u>ayrick Peak); 5 – E (<u>E</u>den Woods); 6 – M (<u>M</u>erryfield Campsite). When you put all these letter together you get the word 'MAYHEM'!

Glossary

aerial overhead, from the sky

continents largest land masses in the world. Except for Antarctica, each continent is divided into different countries.

erode when rocks or land are worn away by wind, water, ice, or by people

glacier giant mass of ice that flows downhill, a permanently frozen river

gradient the steepness of a slope

habitat place or environment where groups of animals and plants live

loch word for lake in Scotland

moorland high, exposed area of land covered with tough, low-growing plants, such as heather

National Parks large areas of countryside in the UK that are protected by law

Ordnance Survey map-making organization that makes maps that cover the whole of the UK

peak highest point of a mountain (also called the summit)

permanent features things that are always in the same place in a landscape, such as bridges or roads

pollution when water, air, or soil are made dirty or poisonous by people's waste

range group of mountains

reservoir lake formed by damming a river to store water that can be piped to settlements

ridge long narrow peak of rock on a hill or mountain or on a mountain range

rocky outcrop patch of hard rock left sticking out when softer rock around it has been eroded away

satellite scientific object that orbits the Earth in space and sends out TV signals or takes photographs

scree small, loose stones covering a mountain slope, broken from the rocks above

summit top of a mountain (also called a peak)

surveyors people who measure things on the ground and accurately record the positions of natural and man-made features

tourism industry that attracts and looks after the needs of tourists

valley deep groove between mountains, usually made by a river or a glacier

Find out more

Books

Wild Habitats: Mountains and Hills, Louise and Richard Spilsbury (Heinemann Library, 2004)

Philip's Junior School Atlas (4th edn), (Heinemann, Rigby, Ginn, 2003)

Websites

You can play games, get homework help and learn more about using maps on the Ordnance Survey Mapzone site:
www.ordnancesurvey.co.uk/mapzone

You can also take a virtual flight over Ben Nevis! Look under 'Flythroughs' in the list of free options on the Ordnance Survey website.

The global eye website has a 'Focus on Mountains' section featuring activities, information, and case studies about some famous mountain ranges of the world:
www.globaleye.org.uk/primary

You can see 360° pictures of mountains in the Pennines and Lake District:
www.virtualcumbria.net

Check out the geography section on the Heinemann Explore website to find out even more about maps!
www.heinemannexplore.co.uk

Have fun with maps in the future – you should never get lost again!

Index

aerial photographs 8, 13, 18, 22
aerial view 4

Ben Nevis 6, 14–15

Cadair Idris 17
colours 9
compass directions 16
contour lines 12, 13, 15, 28

distance, measuring 19, 28
drawing a map 5

erosion 8, 10, 23
Everest 24

glaciers 8
globe 24
gradient 12
gradient arrows 28
grid references 16, 17, 28
grid squares 16, 19, 28

habitat destruction 25
Hardknott Pass 18, 19
height 6, 9, 13
hills 6

ice and snow 6, 7, 14

key (legend) 11

Lake District 18–19
lakes 8, 9, 15
lochs 8

map skills, testing 26–7
moorland 6
mountain features 6–7
mountain ranges 8, 14, 23, 24, 25

National Parks 18, 20

Ordnance Survey maps 15, 17, 19, 21, 28

paths 13, 14, 15
peak (summit) 6, 7, 12, 14, 15, 20, 24
permanent features 5, 8
pollution 23, 25

ridges 8
rivers and streams 8, 9, 10, 15, 19, 25
rocky outcrops 10, 15, 19

safety 5, 14
satellite photographs 22
scale 20–1, 28
scree 10, 15
shaded relief maps 9
slopes 12, 28
Snowdon 8, 13, 20, 21
surveyors 22
symbols 10–11, 28

tourism 23
trees and plants 6, 7, 10, 18

UK mountains 22–3

valleys 8, 12, 15

weather forecast maps 20
world mountains 24–5

Titles in the Mapping the UK series include :

Hardback : 0431013233

Hardback : 043101325X

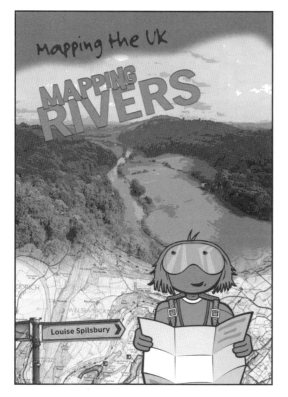

Hardback : 0431013225

Hardback : 0431013241

Find out about other titles from Heinemann Library on our website www.heinemann.co.uk/library